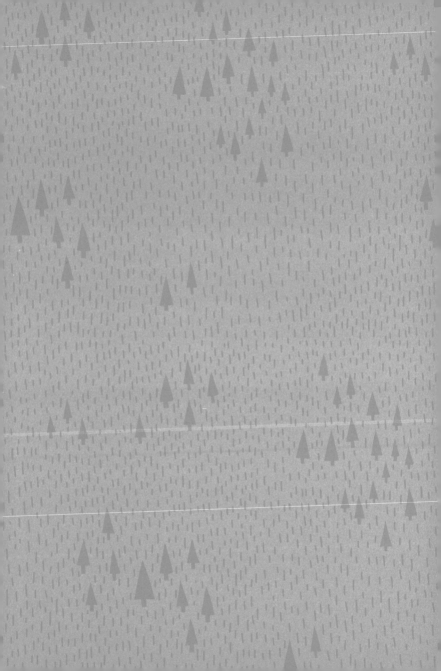

GET OUTSIDE

A Journal
for Refreshing Your
Spirit in Nature

THESE ADVENTURES BELONG TO

_____

_____

Ink &
Willow

I love to think of nature as an unlimited broadcasting station, through which God speaks to us every hour, if only we will tune in.

—GEORGE WASHINGTON CARVER

INTRODUCTION

As Robert Frost once wrote, sometimes taking the road less traveled can make all the difference. We couldn't agree more! We are glad you've decided to take what may be your first steps to finding God in nature with us. Whether you're new to outdoor adventure, an avid weekend trekker, or a wilderness expert, we share your enthusiasm and hope this book will enhance your experiences.

In the pages that follow, you will find an interactive activity log, guided journaling pages, inspiring quotes from nature lovers throughout the ages, as well as blank pages for sketching or posting photos of your adventures. Plus, we couldn't resist including additional practical features such as:

* how to read the clouds
* top outdoor attractions for each U.S. state
* tips for navigating by the stars
* ways to improve your nature photography
* and much more!

Remember, every journey begins with a single step. May each destination you encounter expand your worldview and help you see the fingerprints of God everywhere you look.

DATE

LOCATION

ACTIVITY TYPE

RATING

MEMORIES & IMPRESSIONS

DATE

LOCATION

ACTIVITY TYPE

RATING

MEMORIES & IMPRESSIONS

DATE | LOCATION

ACTIVITY TYPE | RATING

MEMORIES & IMPRESSIONS

DATE | LOCATION

ACTIVITY TYPE | RATING

MEMORIES & IMPRESSIONS

DATE

LOCATION

ACTIVITY TYPE

RATING

MEMORIES & IMPRESSIONS

DATE

LOCATION

ACTIVITY TYPE

RATING

MEMORIES & IMPRESSIONS

DATE

LOCATION

ACTIVITY TYPE

RATING

MEMORIES & IMPRESSIONS

DATE

LOCATION

ACTIVITY TYPE

RATING

MEMORIES & IMPRESSIONS

DATE | LOCATION

ACTIVITY TYPE | RATING

MEMORIES & IMPRESSIONS

DATE | LOCATION

ACTIVITY TYPE | RATING

MEMORIES & IMPRESSIONS

DATE

LOCATION

ACTIVITY TYPE

RATING

MEMORIES & IMPRESSIONS

DATE

LOCATION

ACTIVITY TYPE

RATING

MEMORIES & IMPRESSIONS

DATE

LOCATION

ACTIVITY TYPE

RATING

MEMORIES & IMPRESSIONS

DATE

LOCATION

ACTIVITY TYPE

RATING

MEMORIES & IMPRESSIONS

DATE

LOCATION

ACTIVITY TYPE

RATING

MEMORIES & IMPRESSIONS

DATE

LOCATION

ACTIVITY TYPE

RATING

MEMORIES & IMPRESSIONS

DATE | LOCATION

ACTIVITY TYPE | RATING

MEMORIES & IMPRESSIONS

DATE | LOCATION

ACTIVITY TYPE | RATING

MEMORIES & IMPRESSIONS

DATE | LOCATION

ACTIVITY TYPE | RATING

MEMORIES & IMPRESSIONS

DATE | LOCATION

ACTIVITY TYPE | RATING

MEMORIES & IMPRESSIONS

Take some time to be quiet and still while you are walking through nature. Write down your thoughts and insights. Do you sense God speaking to you? If so, write down those things as well.

— ⚘ —

Everybody needs beauty . . . places to play in
and pray in where nature may heal and cheer
and give strength to the body and soul alike.

—JOHN MUIR

Find something
ordinary around
you. Now describe
its beauty.

———— 🌿 ————

The earth is what we all have in common.

—WENDELL BARRY

What is your favorite
season and why?

To sit in the shade on a fine day,
and look upon verdure is the most
perfect refreshment.

—JANE AUSTEN

If you take the time to notice, your senses come alive when you're outside in nature. Describe what you can see, smell, hear, feel, or taste.

— ✳ —

My soul can find no staircase to Heaven
unless it be through Earth's loveliness.

—MICHELANGELO

What does the beauty
of nature reveal
to you about God?

_____

Like music and art, love of nature is a
common language that can transcend
political or social boundaries.

—JIMMY CARTER

Take a silent walk or hike in nature and then write about your experience. What did you notice without the noise of conversation or other distractions?

_____

_____

_____

_____

_____

_____

_____

_____

_____

_____

_____

_____

_____

_____

_____

The best remedy for those who are afraid,
lonely, or unhappy is to go outside, somewhere
where they can be quiet, alone with the
heavens, nature, and God. Because only then
does one feel that all is as it should be and
that God wishes to see people happy, amidst
the simple beauty of nature.

—ANNE FRANK

How might you be
more attentive to the
natural world in your
everyday life, whether
you live in a big city
or small town?

— 🌿 —

And into the forest I go to lose
my mind and find my soul.

—JOHN MUIR

What are the top three
outdoor destinations
that you hope to visit in
your lifetime?

___ ✿ ___

In the beginning God created
the heavens and the earth.

—GENESIS 1:1

Describe an outdoor
experience or
adventure that made
a lasting impression
on you.

— ⚘ —

_____

_____

_____

_____

_____

_____

_____

_____

_____

_____

_____

_____

_____

_____

_____

_____

_____

_____

_____

_____

_____

_____

The earth has music for those who listen.

—WILLIAM SHAKESPEARE

What is your first
recollection of being
in nature?

———— 🌿 ————

_____

_____

_____

_____

_____

_____

_____

_____

_____

_____

_____

_____

_____

_____

_____

_____

_____

_____

God writes the gospel not in the Bible
alone, but also on trees, and in the flowers
and clouds and stars.

—MARTIN LUTHER

Describe your biggest
outdoor mishap.

——— 🌿 ———

There is a way that nature speaks, that land speaks. Most of the time we are simply not patient enough, quiet enough, to pay attention to the story.

—LINDA HOGAN

Can you point to a
time when you first
became passionate
about nature? What
caused this?

——— 🌿 ———

_____

_____

_____

_____

_____

_____

_____

_____

_____

_____

_____

_____

_____

_____

_____

_____

_____

_____

_____

_____

_____

Man's heart away from nature becomes hard.

—STANDING BEAR

Is there a place
where you feel closest
to God? What takes
you back there?

— 🌿 —

_____

_____

_____

_____

_____

_____

_____

_____

_____

_____

_____

_____

_____

_____

_____

_____

_____

_____

_____

_____

_____

_____

_____

As long as I live, I'll hear waterfalls and
birds and winds sing. I'll interpret the rocks,
learn the language of flood, storm, and
the avalanche. I'll acquaint myself with the
glaciers and wild gardens, and get as near
the heart of the world as I can.

—JOHN MUIR

Record a few thoughts
on your favorite
book about nature
or one that you love
to read in nature.

You alone are the Lord. You made the
skies and the heavens and all the stars.
You made the earth and the seas and
everything in them. You preserve them all,
and the angels of heaven worship you.

—NEHEMIAH 9:6

What do you feel
or experience in nature
that you lack
in everyday life?

—— 🌿 ——

We need to find God and God cannot be found in noise and restlessness. God is the friend of silence. See how nature—trees, flowers, grass—grows in silence; see the stars, the moon, the sun, how they move in silence. . . . We need silence to be able to touch souls.

—MOTHER TERESA

Go outside and open
the Bible to a random
passage. What did
you learn or discover?

— ✺ —

_____

_____

_____

_____

_____

_____

_____

_____

_____

_____

_____

_____

_____

_____

_____

_____

_____

_____

_____

_____

_____

Nothing is more beautiful than the loveliness
of the woods before sunrise.

—GEORGE WASHINGTON CARVER

What holds you
back from engaging
with nature more
often? How can you
change that?

_____

_____

_____

_____

_____

_____

_____

_____

_____

_____

_____

_____

_____

_____

_____

_____

_____

_____

_____

_____

_____

On earth there is no heaven,
but there are pieces of it.

—JULES RENARD

What changes do you
notice in yourself after
you've spent time in
a remote place without
devices or cell service?

The beauty of the natural world
lies in the details.

—NATALIE ANGIER

Describe one of your
favorite recent hikes or
outdoor adventures.

—— 🌿 ——

_____

_____

_____

_____

_____

_____

_____

_____

_____

_____

_____

_____

_____

_____

_____

_____

_____

If nature had never awakened certain
longings in me, huge areas of what I can now
mean by "love" of God would never, so far as
I can see, have existed.

—C. S. LEWIS

What fresh outdoor
scents do you love
the most?

Keep your eyes on the stars, and
your feet on the ground.

—THEODORE ROOSEVELT

Plan your next hike or
outdoor adventure.

— 🌿 —

The whole world is a series of miracles . . . but we're
so used to them we call them ordinary things.

—HANS CHRISTIAN ANDERSEN

Is there a book, song, or film that has deepened your appreciation of nature? In what ways?

In nature, nothing is perfect and everything
is perfect. Trees can be contorted, bent in
weird ways, and they're still beautiful.

—ALICE WALKER

In what ways
can you experience
nature daily?

— 🌿 —

Not all those who wander are lost.

—J. R. R. TOLKIEN

Describe a moment
when you felt firsthand
the wildness of nature.

— ✺ —

_____

_____

_____

_____

_____

_____

_____

_____

_____

_____

_____

_____

_____

_____

_____

_____

_____

He holds in his hands the depths of the
earth and the mightiest mountains.
The sea belongs to him, for he made it.
His hands formed the dry land, too.

—PSALM 95:4–5

Have you ever been
caught in a downpour
or thunderstorm? If so,
what happened?

— ※ —

_____

_____

_____

_____

_____

_____

_____

_____

_____

_____

_____

_____

_____

_____

_____

_____

_____

_____

_____

_____

_____

I cannot endure to waste anything so precious
as autumnal sunshine by staying in the house.

—NATHANIEL HAWTHORNE

Sit somewhere in
nature and write down
what you see as though
you were an author
describing a setting for
a novel.

———— 🌿 ————

A weed is no more than a flower in disguise.

—JAMES RUSSELL LOWELL

What do you love
about your own
backyard or garden?

———— 🌿 ————

Study nature, love nature, stay close to
nature. It will never fail you.

—FRANK LLOYD WRIGHT

If you could drop your house into any national park, which one would you choose and why?

—— 🌿 ——

_____

_____

_____

_____

_____

_____

_____

_____

_____

_____

_____

_____

_____

_____

_____

_____

_____

_____

_____

Wildness reminds us what it means to be
human, what we are connected to rather
than what we are separate from.

—TERRY TEMPEST WILLIAMS

Which do you prefer,
beaches or mountains?
Why?

———— ⚘ ————

Adopt the pace of nature: her secret is patience.

—RALPH WALDO EMERSON

Go for a prayer walk
and then jot down
a few thoughts about
your experience.

———— 🌿 ————

_____

_____

_____

_____

_____

_____

_____

_____

_____

_____

_____

_____

_____

_____

_____

_____

_____

_____

_____

_____

_____

_____

_____

_____

I firmly believe that nature brings
solace in all troubles.

—ANNE FRANK

What are some of your
favorite nature sounds?
Why?

— 🌿 —

Of all the paths you take in life, make
sure a few of them are dirt.

—JOHN MUIR

Go outside and stand still for a few minutes. What one aspect of nature stood out to you during that time?

— ⚘ —

I will meditate on your majestic, glorious
splendor and your wonderful miracles.

—PSALM 145:5

Describe one of your
favorite places to
watch a sunset or
sunrise. What makes
it so special?

———— 🌿 ————

Sunset is still my favorite color,
and rainbow is second.

—MATTIE STEPANEK

What are you most
thankful for in nature?

I've always regarded nature as the
clothing of God.

—ALAN HOVHANESS

What differences do
you notice when you
experience nature alone
versus in a group?

———— 🌿 ————

_____

_____

_____

_____

_____

_____

_____

_____

_____

_____

_____

_____

_____

_____

_____

_____

_____

_____

_____

_____

_____

_____

The heavens declare the glory of God; the
skies proclaim the work of his hands.

—PSALM 19:1

Change up your routine
by turning a meal
you normally eat
inside into an outdoor
picnic. How does the
experience affect you?

———— 🌿 ————

_____

_____

_____

_____

_____

_____

_____

_____

_____

_____

_____

_____

_____

_____

_____

_____

_____

_____

_____

_____

_____

_____

_____

_____

_____

_____

_____

_____

_____

_____

_____

_____

_____

_____

_____

_____

_____

_____

_____

_____

_____

Nature is a volume of which God is the author.

—WILLIAM HARVEY

Find a river or lake to
sit by while you read
Psalm 23, Psalm 42,
or one of the passages
about the Red Sea or
the Jordan River. Write
down any new insights
that stand out to you.

———— ⚘ ————

Those who contemplate the beauty of the
earth find reserves of strength that will endure
as long as life lasts. There is something infinitely
healing in the repeated refrains of nature—
the assurance that dawn comes after night,
and spring after winter.

—RACHEL CARSON

Describe your favorite
outdoor space from
your childhood.

———— ✿ ————

_____

_____

_____

_____

_____

_____

_____

_____

_____

_____

_____

_____

_____

_____

_____

_____

_____

_____

_____

_____

_____

The best thing one can do when it's
raining is to let it rain.

—HENRY WADSWORTH LONGFELLOW

To date, what was
your most epic
adventure? What
made it so amazing?

— ✦ —

Doth not all nature around me praise God? If I were
silent, I should be an exception to the universe.

—CHARLES SPURGEON

Go stargazing with a friend or family member. As you watch for shooting stars or look for constellations, talk about what God is doing in your lives or simply listen to a favorite worship album in silence. Describe the experience.

_____

_____

_____

_____

_____

_____

_____

_____

_____

_____

_____

_____

_____

_____

_____

_____

_____

_____

_____

_____

_____

_____

_____

_____

_____

_____

_____

_____

_____

_____

_____

_____

_____

_____

_____

_____

_____

_____

_____

_____

_____

_____

_____

_____

_____

Between every two pines is a doorway
to a new world.

—JOHN MUIR

#GETOUTSIDE

No matter where you live or travel in the United States, there are countless outdoor adventures to enjoy. As you plan your next nature hike or wilderness excursion, consider visiting the following national and state parks as well as the other top outdoor destinations. Although this is by no means an exhaustive list, each state contains beautiful settings where you can experience the natural world.

ALABAMA

- ☐ Bankhead National Forest
- ☐ Conecuh National Forest
- ☐ Little River Canyon National Preserve
- ☐ Natchez Trace National Scenic Trail
- ☐ Tuskegee National Forest

ALASKA

- ☐ Denali National Park
- ☐ Gates of the Arctic National Park
- ☐ Glacier Bay National Park
- ☐ Kenai Fjords National Park
- ☐ Wrangell–St. Elias National Park

ARIZONA

- ☐ Grand Canyon National Park
- ☐ Monument Valley Navajo Tribal Park
- ☐ Petrified Forest National Park
- ☐ Saguaro National Park
- ☐ Sunset Crater National Monuments
- ☐ Vermillion Cliffs National Monument

ARKANSAS

- ☐ Buffalo National River Park
- ☐ Hot Springs National Park
- ☐ Ouachita National Forest
- ☐ Ozark–St. Francis National Forests
- ☐ Sylamore National Forest

CALIFORNIA

- ☐ Death Valley National Park
- ☐ Joshua Tree National Park
- ☐ Muir Woods National Monument
- ☐ Point Reyes National Seashore
- ☐ Sequoia & Kings Canyon National Parks
- ☐ Yosemite National Park

COLORADO

- ☐ Garden of the Gods
- ☐ Great Sand Dunes National Park
- ☐ Mesa Verde National Park
- ☐ Pike National Forest
- ☐ Rocky Mountain National Park
- ☐ San Juan Skyway Scenic Byway

CONNECTICUT

- ☐ Gillette Castle State Park
- ☐ Hammonasset Beach State Park
- ☐ Kent Falls State Park
- ☐ Sleeping Giant State Park
- ☐ White Memorial Foundation and Conservation Center

DELAWARE

- ☐ Cape Henlopen State Park
- ☐ Delaware Seashore State Park
- ☐ Fenwick Island State Park
- ☐ White Clay Creek State Park

FLORIDA

- ☐ Apalachicola National Forest
- ☐ Dry Tortugas National Park
- ☐ Everglades National Park
- ☐ Gulf Islands National Seashore
- ☐ John Pennekamp Coral Reef State Park
- ☐ Juniper Prairie Wilderness

GEORGIA

- ☐ Black Rock Mountain State Park
- ☐ Chattahoochee-Oconee National Forest
- ☐ Crooked River State Park
- ☐ Etowah Indian Mounds Historic Site
- ☐ Franklin D. Roosevelt State Park

HAWAII

- ☐ Haleakala National Park
- ☐ Hawaii Volcanoes National Park
- ☐ Makena State Park
- ☐ Na Pali Coast State Park
- ☐ Pu'uhonua o Hōnaunau National Historical Park

IDAHO

- ☐ City of Rocks National Reserve
- ☐ Craters of the Moon National Monument and Reserve
- ☐ Frank Church River of No Return Wilderness
- ☐ Hagerman Fossil Beds National Monument
- ☐ Sawtooth National Forest

ILLINOIS

- ☐ Cohokia Mounds State Historic Site
- ☐ Midewin National Tallgrass Prairie
- ☐ Shawnee National Forest
- ☐ Starved Rock State Park
- ☐ Volo Bog State National Area

INDIANA

- ☐ Clifty Falls State Park
- ☐ Hoosier National Forest
- ☐ Indiana Dunes State Park
- ☐ Marengo Cave
- ☐ McCormick Creek State Park

IOWA

- ☐ Effigy Mounds National Monument
- ☐ Lacey-Keosauqua State Park
- ☐ Lewis & Clark National Historic Trail
- ☐ Loess Hills National Scenic Byway
- ☐ Wildcat Den State Park

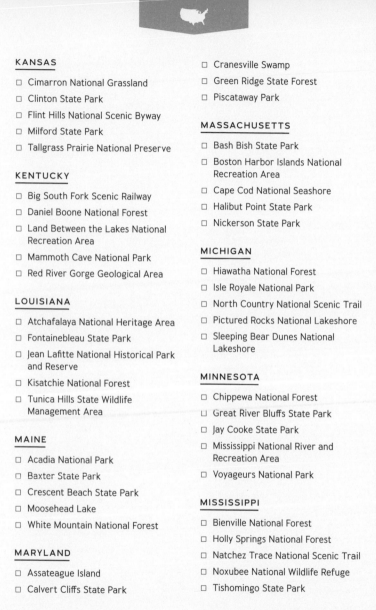

KANSAS

- ☐ Cimarron National Grassland
- ☐ Clinton State Park
- ☐ Flint Hills National Scenic Byway
- ☐ Milford State Park
- ☐ Tallgrass Prairie National Preserve

KENTUCKY

- ☐ Big South Fork Scenic Railway
- ☐ Daniel Boone National Forest
- ☐ Land Between the Lakes National Recreation Area
- ☐ Mammoth Cave National Park
- ☐ Red River Gorge Geological Area

LOUISIANA

- ☐ Atchafalaya National Heritage Area
- ☐ Fontainebleau State Park
- ☐ Jean Lafitte National Historical Park and Reserve
- ☐ Kisatchie National Forest
- ☐ Tunica Hills State Wildlife Management Area

MAINE

- ☐ Acadia National Park
- ☐ Baxter State Park
- ☐ Crescent Beach State Park
- ☐ Moosehead Lake
- ☐ White Mountain National Forest

MARYLAND

- ☐ Assateague Island
- ☐ Calvert Cliffs State Park
- ☐ Cranesville Swamp
- ☐ Green Ridge State Forest
- ☐ Piscataway Park

MASSACHUSETTS

- ☐ Bash Bish State Park
- ☐ Boston Harbor Islands National Recreation Area
- ☐ Cape Cod National Seashore
- ☐ Halibut Point State Park
- ☐ Nickerson State Park

MICHIGAN

- ☐ Hiawatha National Forest
- ☐ Isle Royale National Park
- ☐ North Country National Scenic Trail
- ☐ Pictured Rocks National Lakeshore
- ☐ Sleeping Bear Dunes National Lakeshore

MINNESOTA

- ☐ Chippewa National Forest
- ☐ Great River Bluffs State Park
- ☐ Jay Cooke State Park
- ☐ Mississippi National River and Recreation Area
- ☐ Voyageurs National Park

MISSISSIPPI

- ☐ Bienville National Forest
- ☐ Holly Springs National Forest
- ☐ Natchez Trace National Scenic Trail
- ☐ Noxubee National Wildlife Refuge
- ☐ Tishomingo State Park

MISSOURI

- ☐ Ha Ha Tonka State Park
- ☐ Mark Twain National Forest
- ☐ Roaring River State Park
- ☐ Table Rock Lake
- ☐ Talking Rocks Cavern

MONTANA

- ☐ Beaverhead-Deerlodge National Forest
- ☐ Custer National Forest
- ☐ Flathead National Forest
- ☐ Glacier National Park
- ☐ Helena National Forest
- ☐ Yellowstone National Park

NEBRASKA

- ☐ Ashfall Fossil Beds State Historical Park
- ☐ Fort Robinson State Park
- ☐ Nebraska National Forest
- ☐ Oglala National Grassland
- ☐ Platte River State Park

NEVADA

- ☐ Gold Butte National Monument
- ☐ Great Basin National Park
- ☐ Lake Mead National Recreation Area
- ☐ Pony Express Historic Trail
- ☐ Red Rock Canyon National Conservation Area

NEW HAMPSHIRE

- ☐ Franconia Notch State Park
- ☐ Pawtuckaway State Park
- ☐ Rhododendron State Park
- ☐ Sculptured Rocks Natural Area
- ☐ White Mountain National Forest

NEW JERSEY

- ☐ Bass River State Forest
- ☐ Cape May Point State Park
- ☐ Long Beach Island
- ☐ Paterson Great Falls National Historical Park
- ☐ Pinelands National Reserve
- ☐ Stokes State Forest

NEW MEXICO

- ☐ Bandelier National Monument
- ☐ Bosque del Apache Wildlife Refuge
- ☐ Carlsbad Caverns National Park
- ☐ Chaco Culture National Historical Park
- ☐ Kasha-Katuwe Tent Rocks National Monument
- ☐ White Sands National Monument

NEW YORK

- ☐ Buttermilk Falls State Park
- ☐ Finger Lakes National Forest
- ☐ Taughannock Falls State Park
- ☐ Watkins Glen State Park

NORTH CAROLINA

- ☐ Croatan National Forest
- ☐ Blue Ridge Parkway
- ☐ Great Smoky Mountains National Park
- ☐ Nantahala National Forest
- ☐ Outer Banks
- ☐ Pisgah National Forest

NORTH DAKOTA

- ☐ Dakota Prairie Grasslands
- ☐ Little Missouri State Park
- ☐ Maah Daah Hey Trail
- ☐ Pembina Gorge State Recreation Area
- ☐ Theodore Roosevelt National Park

OHIO

- ☐ Cuyahoga Valley National Park
- ☐ Hocking Hills State Park
- ☐ Lake Erie State Park
- ☐ Ohio Caverns
- ☐ Wayne National Forest

OKLAHOMA

- ☐ Beavers Bend State Park
- ☐ Black Kettle and McClellan Creek National Grasslands
- ☐ Ouachita National Forest
- ☐ Robbers Cave State Park
- ☐ Wichita Mountains Wildlife Refuge

OREGON

- ☐ Columbia River Gorge National Scenic Area
- ☐ Crater Lake National Park
- ☐ Deschutes National Forest
- ☐ Ecola State Park
- ☐ Mount Hood National Forest
- ☐ Smith Rock State Park

PENNSYLVANIA

- ☐ Allegheny National Forest
- ☐ Delaware Water Gap National Recreation Area
- ☐ Independence National Historical Park
- ☐ Ohiopyle State Park
- ☐ Presque Isle State Park

RHODE ISLAND

- ☐ Blackstone River and Canal Heritage State Park
- ☐ Block Island
- ☐ Colt State Park
- ☐ Ocean Drive Historic District
- ☐ Sachuest Point National Wildlife Refuge

SOUTH CAROLINA

- ☐ Cherry Grove Beach
- ☐ Congaree National Park
- ☐ Francis Marion and Sumpter National Forests
- ☐ Hilton Head Island

SOUTH DAKOTA

- ☐ Badlands National Park
- ☐ Black Hills National Forest
- ☐ Buffalo Gap National Grassland
- ☐ Custer State Park
- ☐ Jewel Cave National Monument
- ☐ Mount Rushmore National Monument

TENNESSEE

- ☐ Cherokee National Forest
- ☐ Cummins Falls State Park
- ☐ Falls Creek State Park
- ☐ Great Smoky Mountains National Park
- ☐ Land Between the Lakes National Recreation Area

TEXAS

- ☐ Big Bend National Park
- ☐ Devils River State Natural Area
- ☐ Garner State Park
- ☐ Padre Island National Seashore
- ☐ Palo Duro Canyon

UTAH

- ☐ Arches National Park
- ☐ Bryce Canyon National Park
- ☐ Canyonlands National Park
- ☐ Grand Staircase-Escalante National Monument
- ☐ Uinta-Wasatch-Cache National Forest
- ☐ Zion National Park

VERMONT

- ☐ Green Mountain National Forest
- ☐ Lake Champlain
- ☐ Mount Philo State Park
- ☐ Smugglers Notch State Park
- ☐ Underhill State Park

VIRGINIA

- ☐ False Cape State Park
- ☐ George Washington and Jefferson National Forests
- ☐ Grayson Highlands/Mount Rogers National Recreation Area
- ☐ Great Dismal Swamp National Wildlife Refuge
- ☐ Shenandoah National Park

WASHINGTON

- ☐ Cape Disappointment State Park
- ☐ Mount Rainier National Park
- ☐ Mount St. Helens National Volcanic Monument
- ☐ North Cascades National Park
- ☐ Olympic National Park
- ☐ San Juan Islands National Monument

WEST VIRGINIA

- ☐ Blackwater Falls State Park
- ☐ Coopers Rock State Forest
- ☐ Monongahela National Forest
- ☐ New River Gorge National River

WISCONSIN

- ☐ Apostle Islands National Lakeshore
- ☐ Chequamegon-Nicolet National Forest
- ☐ Devil's Lake State Park
- ☐ High Cliff State Park
- ☐ Pattison State Park

WYOMING

- ☐ Bighorn National Forest
- ☐ Bridger-Teton National Forest
- ☐ Devils Tower National Monument
- ☐ Flaming Gorge National Recreation Area
- ☐ Grand Teton National Park
- ☐ Yellowstone National Park

MY TRAVEL BUCKET LIST

Are there places you've always dreamed of visiting? In the space below, create your own bucket list of outdoor destinations you plan to see.

☐ _____   ☐ _____

☐ _____   ☐ _____

☐ _____   ☐ _____

☐ _____   ☐ _____

☐ _____   ☐ _____

☐ _____   ☐ _____

☐ _____   ☐ _____

☐ _____   ☐ _____

☐ _____   ☐ _____

☐ _____   ☐ _____

☐ _____   ☐ _____

☐ _____   ☐ _____

☐ _____   ☐ _____

☐ _____   ☐ _____

☐ _____   ☐ _____

☐ _____   ☐ _____

☐ _____   ☐ _____

☐ _____   ☐ _____

☐ _____   ☐ _____

☐ _____   ☐ _____

☐ _____   ☐ _____

☐ _____   ☐ _____

☐ _____   ☐ _____

☐ _____   ☐ _____

☐ _____   ☐ _____

☐ _____   ☐ _____

☐ _____   ☐ _____

☐ _____   ☐ _____

☐ _____   ☐ _____

☐ _____   ☐ _____

☐ _____   ☐ _____

☐ _____   ☐ _____

☐ _____   ☐ _____

☐ _____   ☐ _____

☐ _____   ☐ _____

☐ _____   ☐ _____

☐ _____   ☐ _____

☐ _____   ☐ _____

☐ _____   ☐ _____

☐ _____   ☐ _____

☐ _____   ☐ _____

OUTDOOR ATTRACTIONS
OFF THE BEATEN PATH

If you're looking for hidden gems or out-of-the-way destinations
that many travelers miss, check out the following list.

THE CANAL WALK AND WHITE RIVER STATE PARK, INDIANA

Located in downtown
Indianapolis, this is not your
typical park or waterway.
With options for the fitness
junky and culture seeker alike,
this scenic urban state park
has much to explore.

TALLULAH GORGE STATE PARK, GEORGIA

Tallulah Gorge is a two-mile-long
gorge that drops nearly 1000 feet
over near vertical walls and is one
of North Georgia's most beautiful,
rugged places. There are many
hiking and biking trails available,
including those that take you
to Tallulah Falls, a series of six
waterfalls plunging into the gorge.

RAINBOW FALLS, COLORADO

This gorgeous hiking trail located
in Manitou Springs, just west of
downtown Colorado Springs,
takes you to the waterfall and a
historic bridge. The bridge, which
crosses the creek at the falls, was
built in 1932 and is noteworthy
because of its open-arching
structural design.

THE ROAD TO NOWHERE, NORTH CAROLINA

This scenic six-mile highway takes you into Great Smoky Mountains National Park and ends at the mouth of a tunnel. Providing views of Fontana Lake and access to several hiking trails, The Road to Nowhere (called Lakeview Drive on maps) is particularly lovely in the fall.

SEVEN BRIDGES ROAD, ALABAMA

Immortalized in the song by Steve Young made famous by the Eagles, this country road (now officially known as Woodley Road) crosses seven bridges on its way out of Montgomery.

PARADISE COVE, COLORADO

Just outside of Cripple Creek, a short half-mile hike leads to this secluded swimming hole surrounded by granite rocks. Locals know it as a great spot for cliff jumping into the small, deep pool fed by a waterfall.

WILDWOOD REGIONAL PARK, CALIFORNIA

Containing diverse landscapes such as sweeping grasslands and prominent ridges and peaks, this park is one of the most fascinating in the L.A. area. Located in Ventura County, this beautiful park contains twenty-seven miles of hiking trails.

HAWKSBILL CRAG TRAIL, ARKANSAS

This hiking trail (also known as Whitaker Point Trail) leads to one of the most photographed locations in Arkansas. With scenic views of the beautiful Ozarks and an easy to moderate difficulty rating, this is an amazing location to explore.

DEVIL'S GULCH PARK, SOUTH DAKOTA

According to local legend, Jesse James evaded capture by leaping over this ravine near Garretson in September 1876 after his gang tried and failed to rob a bank in Minnesota. Now named Devil's Gulch Park, it features a metal footbridge over the deep pool below.

TOADSTOOL GEOLOGIC PARK, NEBRASKA

Located in far northwestern Nebraska, this park is named after its unusual rock formations. Among the rocks, visitors often find fossil remains of tortoises, rhinos, saber-tooth cats, three-toed horses, and camels.

NORTH CLEAR CREEK FALLS, COLORADO

This 100-foot waterfall in the southwest part of the state is a fantastic place to pull off for a picnic or just to take in the views of this dramatic waterfall.

KLYDE WARREN PARK, TEXAS

This public park in downtown Dallas provides much-needed green space in the middle of the city. With activities and entertainment options for the whole family, this is a vibrant urban park.

CHAPMAN'S MILL, VIRGINIA

Believed to be the tallest stacked stone building in the United States, this is a historic grist mill (also called Beverley Mill) located near Broad Run, Virginia. It was built in 1759 for local farmers who wanted to process and transfer their wheat and corn to the nearby port town of Alexandria.

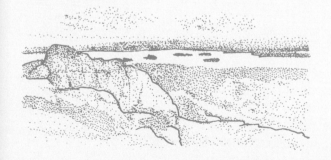

JACOB'S WELL, TEXAS

This perennial karstic spring in the Texas Hill Country has lured locals and visitors for hundreds of years. Daredevils leap into the cool water from a nearby outcropping and divers have explored as far as 100 feet down. Though it can be dangerous for thrill seekers, it's also a beautiful spot to escape the Texas heat.

CADILLAC MOUNTAIN VIEWPOINT, MAINE

Located in the Acadia National Park, Cadillac Mountain is the highest point along the North Atlantic seaboard and the first place in the United States to be touched by the sun's rays every morning. The summit can be reached by hiking or by driving the scenic Summit Road.

CUMBERLAND ISLAND, GEORGIA

An undeveloped barrier island off the southeast coast of Georgia that was once the plantation and retreat of the famous Carnegie family. There are four historic districts on the island and more than 87 structures listed on the National Register of Historic Places. With eighteen miles of isolated and unspoiled beaches as well as maritime forestland, this island has a unique geography and history.

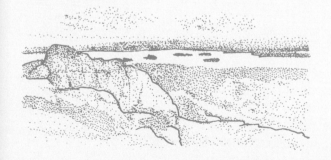

THE DOS AND DON'TS . . .

DO

✔ Research equipment and clothing needs for weather forecast and destination.

✔ Be prepared for an emergency by carrying the following: whistle, knife, extra layers, first aid kit, compass, flashlight, and map.

✔ Drink plenty of water before, during, and after your hike.

✔ Bring high-protein snacks such as granola bars or trail mix.

✔ Study a trail map or app before you leave to familiarize yourself with the area. Take a photo or screenshot of the map so you're not dependent on internet or cell service for directions.

✔ Leave the trails in better condition than you found them.

✔ Carry a fully charged cell phone.

✔ Wear sunscreen, sunglasses, and a hat.

✔ Prevent altitude sickness by consuming plenty of water and carbs, avoiding alcohol, and climbing at a slow and comfortable pace.

. . . OF DAY HIKING

DON'T

✕ Hike alone or leave without letting
someone know where you're going.

✕ Touch if you don't know what it is!

✕ Turn your back on a bear or other wild
animal.

✕ Wear inappropriate shoes.

✕ Attempt to hike an overly strenuous trail
if you're not up to it.

✕ Remove anything from the forest or trail.

✕ Leave litter or other trash behind.

✕ Disturb the land. As much as possible,
refrain from stacking cairns, building fire pits,
or clearing underbrush.

THE TOP TEN
OUTDOOR MYTHS

MYTH #10

Bears attack humans frequently.

TRUTH: The number of bear attacks is greatly exaggerated. There were only ten fatal bear attacks in the US between 2010 and 2016.

MYTH #9

You don't need to drink as much water when enjoying outdoor activities in the winter.

TRUTH: Cold and dry days can make you just as prone to dehydration as hot ones. It's always wise to carry plenty of water with you unless you have a portable water filter.

MYTH #8

Rub two sticks together to start a fire.

TRUTH: Although friction is an effective way to create a flame, you can't just rub any two sticks together. It takes a great deal of patience, practice, and luck to make a fire this way. If you are on an extended outdoor trip, make sure to carry waterproof matches (or regular matches in a waterproof container).

MYTH #7

You should try to suck the venom out of a snakebite.

TRUTH: Snakes strike only when they feel threatened or surprised, so always be on the alert when you spend extended time outside. If you do get bitten, do not try to suck out the venom. Snakebites can be quite deep and venom travels through the bloodstream very quickly, so trying to arrest that process is virtually impossible. In addition, your mouth and saliva are teeming with bacteria that could cause infection if you put it on an open wound. Get to a hospital or emergency room as soon as possible for treatment.

MYTH #6

Drinking alcoholic beverages will warm you up in cold weather.

TRUTH: Liquor is the last thing you should drink in a cold-weather survival scenario. You may feel warmer, but alcohol dilates skin-surface blood vessels and capillaries, which will cause your core to become colder more quickly. Instead, enjoy a hot beverage such as tea or coffee.

MYTH #5

Rub frostbitten skin.

TRUTH: Don't. Ever. Frostbite occurs when ice crystals form in your skin and other tissues. Rubbing the area causes more tissue damage as the ice crystals lacerate new cells. Instead, treat the victim with painkillers as you slowly rewarm the tissue—frostbite hurts!

MYTH #4

Carrying a first-aid kit makes you safe.

TRUTH: Along with supplies, it's essential that you have the knowledge to treat the most common injuries. Consider taking a first-aid course or do some research online beforehand so you know what to do in the case of a cut, burn, or other mishap.

MYTH #3

In a survival scenario, you should drink your own urine to stay hydrated.

TRUTH: Urine is full of the body's waste products. If conditions are grim enough to inspire you to consider urine as a beverage, then you are most likely severely dehydrated. The urine of a dehydrated person should not be reintroduced into the human body under any circumstances. Pee can be handy in other ways: Use it to dampen clothing for evaporative cooling in hot climates. But it's not safe or smart to drink it.

MYTH #2

Moss always grows on the north side of the tree.

TRUTH: Moss tends to grow where conditions are cool and moist. This is frequently on the north side of tree trunks, which often are protected from direct sunlight. However, all sides of the tree are likely to be shaded in the woods, so this directional clue isn't reliable.

MYTH #1

Use a tourniquet if you're bleeding.

TRUTH: Tourniquets are actually very dangerous since they can damage blood vessels, kill tissue, and possibly make amputation necessary. A tourniquet should only be used as a last resort for someone who would otherwise quickly bleed to death.

INFORMATION ADAPTED FROM
THE FOLLOWING SOURCES:

https://urbansurvivalsite.com/20-common-survival-myths/

https://www.outdoorlife.com/articles/survival/2016/04/dead-wrong-26-survival-myths-can-get-you-killed

https://www.outwardbound.org/blog/11-wilderness-backpacking-myths-explained/

https://www.wideopenspaces.com/10-false-myths-grew-hearing/

HOW TO READ THE CLOUDS

Learning to identify different types of cloud formations will help you know what kind of weather to expect when spending extended time outdoors.

ALTOCUMULUS

Lower than cirrus clouds, these clouds have several patchy white or gray layers and look like many small rows of fluffy ripples. They rarely produce rain and instead indicate fair weather.

ALTOSTRATUS

Gray or blue-gray mid-level clouds made up of ice crystals or water droplets, which usually cover the entire sky. Be prepared for precipitation in the form of continuous rain or snow!

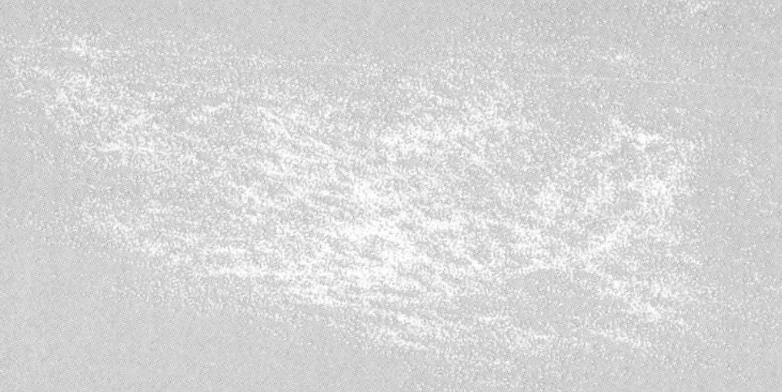

CIRROCUMULUS

These thin, frequently patchy, sheet-like clouds indicate fair but cold weather (unless you live in a tropical region, when they can signal an approaching hurricane).

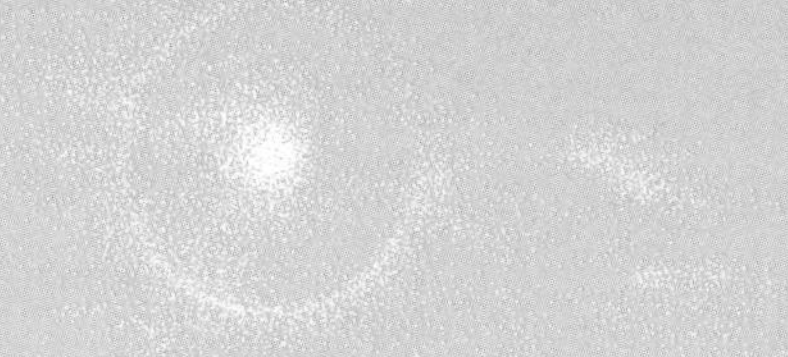

CIRROSTRATUS

Commonly seen in the winter, these thin white clouds cover the sky like a veil and herald the arrival of rain or snow within twenty-four hours.

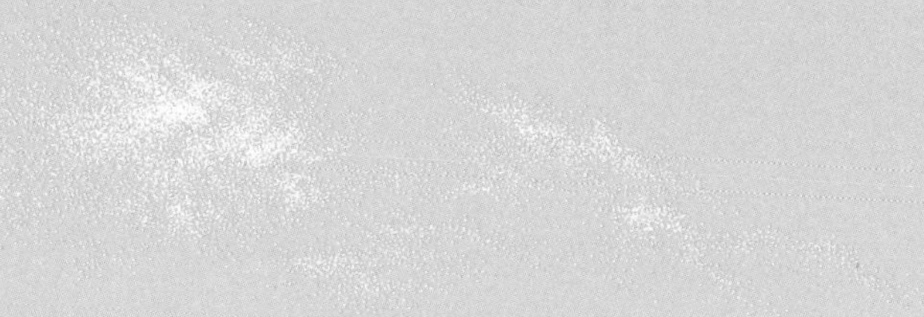

CIRRUS

Delicate, wispy, high-altitude clouds that are made up of ice crystals and are a sign that the weather is about to change.

CUMULUS

These low-altitude clouds look like big white cotton balls in the sky. Study their diverse shapes and sizes, or enjoy the way they create beautiful sunsets, especially since they indicate fair weather.

CUMULONIMBUS

These clouds develop on hot days when warm, moist air rises very high into the sky. From a distance, they resemble huge mountains or towers and they frequently signal stormy weather including rain, hail, and tornadoes.

NIMBOSTRATUS

A sign of gloomy weather, these dark, gray clouds often are thick enough to blot out the sunlight and seem to fade into falling rain or snow.

STRATOCUMULUS

Patchy gray or white clouds that often have a dark honeycomb-like appearance. Weather may be fair now, but there could be storms on the way.

STRATUS

Thin, white sheets that frequently cover the whole sky and can look like fog in the mountains or hills. They are very thin, so they rarely produce much precipitation but they indicate fair, gloomy weather.

INFORMATION ADAPTED FROM "Types of Clouds," SciJinks, https://scijinks.gov/clouds/.

HOW TO NAVIGATE BY THE STARS

Have you ever wondered what you might do if you become lost or disoriented while in a remote area? The instructions below outline a simple technique to finding your way even without Google maps or a compass. You will have to wait for nightfall before using the stars as a navigation aid, but mastering this strategy could save your life someday.

Drive two stakes in the ground about a yard apart. Pick any bright star in the night sky and line it up with the tops of both stakes. Then wait for the star to move out of alignment with the stakes. Earth's rotation from west to east causes the stars in the sky to rotate from east to west. You can tell which direction you're facing by figuring out which way the star has moved relative to its original position. If the star rose, you're facing east but if the star sank, you're facing west. If the star moved to the left, you're facing north and if it moved to the right, you're facing south.

For additional stargazing fun, below are a few of the most commonly visible constellations in the Northern Hemisphere.

INFORMATION ADAPTED FROM "How to Navigate by the Stars," WikiHow, https://www.wikihow.com/Navigate-by-the-Stars.

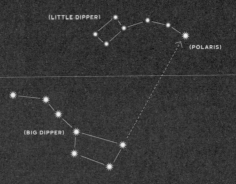

(LITTLE DIPPER)

(POLARIS)

(BIG DIPPER)

THE BIG DIPPER, LITTLE DIPPER, AND POLARIS (OR NORTH STAR)

(PLEIADES)
(TAURUS)
(ORION)

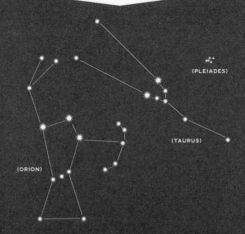

ORION, TAURUS, AND THE PLEIADES

GEMINI (OR THE TWINS)

(POLARIS)
(CASSIOPEIA)
(BIG DIPPER)

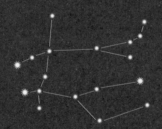

CASSIOPEIA

IDENTIFYING ANIMAL TRACKS

The more time you spend in the great outdoors, the more likely you are to encounter many different animal footprints. Learning to recognize various wild animals by their tracks will help you remain vigilant as you enjoy nature. Note that the following illustrations are not to scale and that front tracks are on the right while hind tracks are on the left.

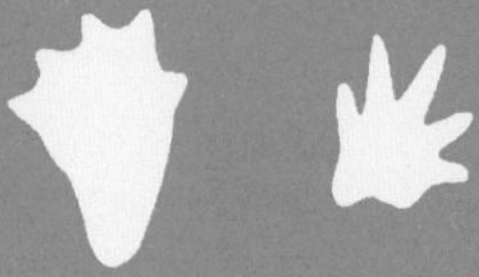

BEAVER

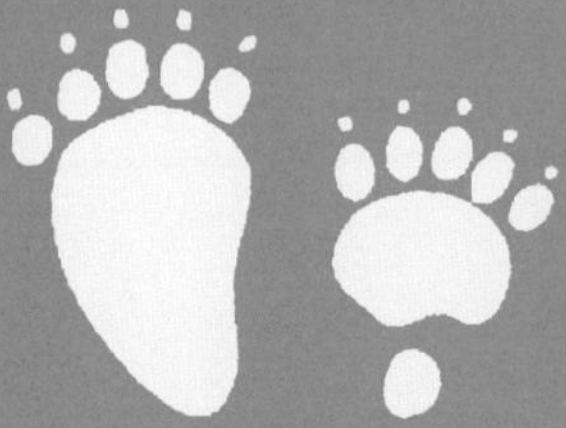

BLACK BEAR

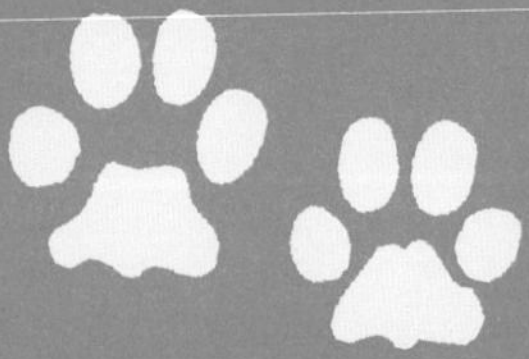

BOBCAT

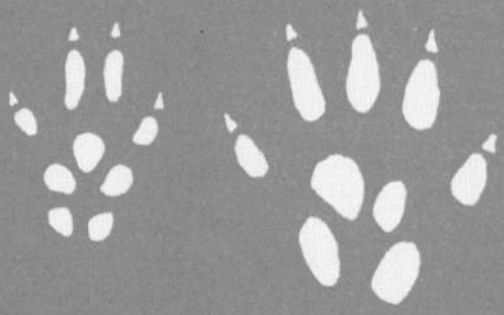

CHIPMUNK

COTTONTAIL RABBIT

COYOTE

GRAY SQUIRREL

GRIZZLY BEAR

MINK

MOOSE

MUSKRAT

OPOSSUM

OTTER

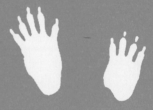

PORCUPINE

RACCOON

RED FOX

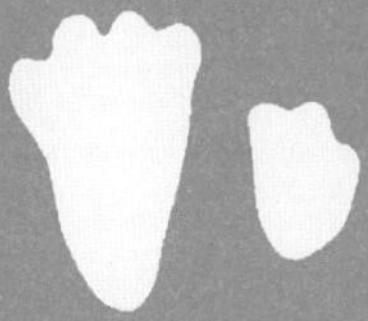

SNOWSHOE HARE

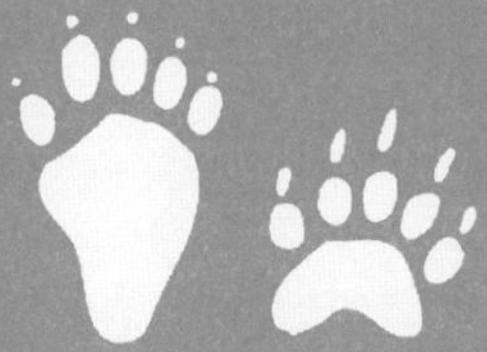

STRIPED SKUNK

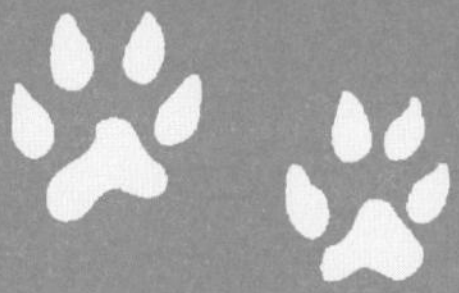

WEASEL

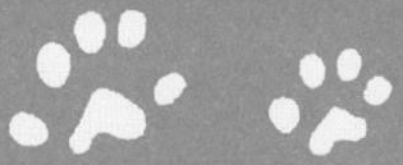

WHITE-FOOTED MOUSE

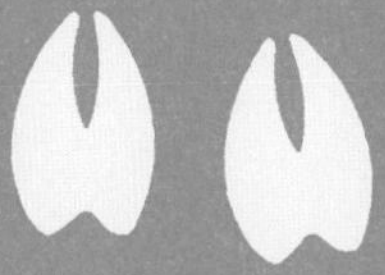

WHITE-TAILED DEER

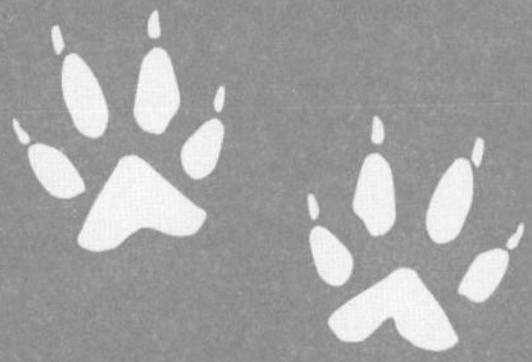

WOLF

IDENTIFYING TREES
BY THEIR LEAVES

This simple foliage identification guide will help you recognize
some of the most common trees throughout North America.

COMMON CONIFEROUS TREES

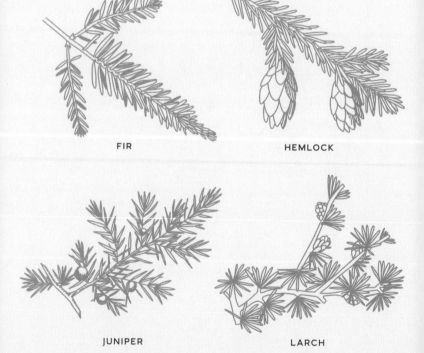

FIR

HEMLOCK

JUNIPER

LARCH

WHITE PINE

PONDEROSA PINE

REDWOOD

SEQUOIA

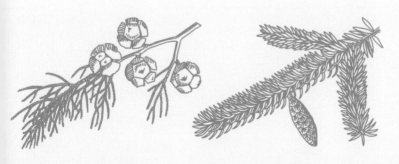

CYPRESS

SPRUCE

COMMON DECIDUOUS TREES

ASPEN

BIRCH

BLACK WALNUT

ELM

GINKGO

HORSE CHESTNUT

SUGAR MAPLE

RED MAPLE

WHITE OAK

RED OAK

SYCAMORE

WHITE ASH

U.S. MOUNTAINS

HOW DO THEY COMPARE?

This illustration gives you an idea of how some of the tallest U.S. mountains compare to Mt. Everest, which is Earth's highest mountain above sea level.

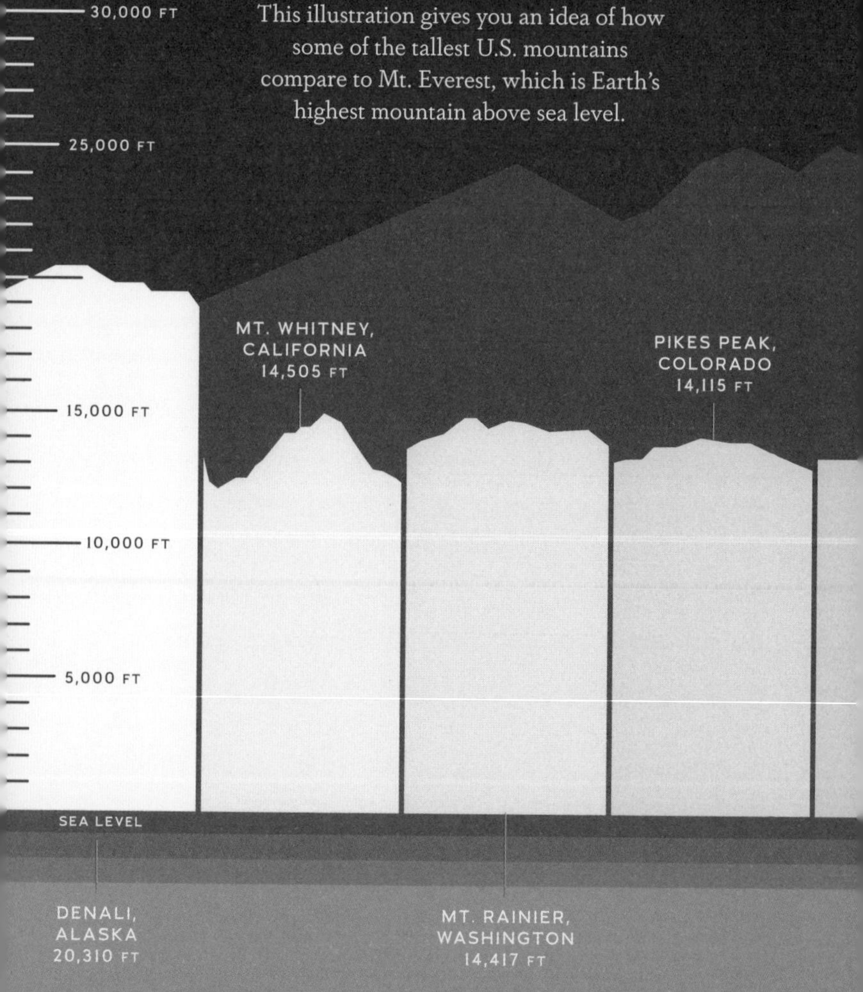

30,000 FT
25,000 FT
15,000 FT
10,000 FT
5,000 FT
SEA LEVEL
MT. WHITNEY, CALIFORNIA 14,505 FT
PIKES PEAK, COLORADO 14,115 FT
DENALI, ALASKA 20,310 FT
MT. RAINIER, WASHINGTON 14,417 FT

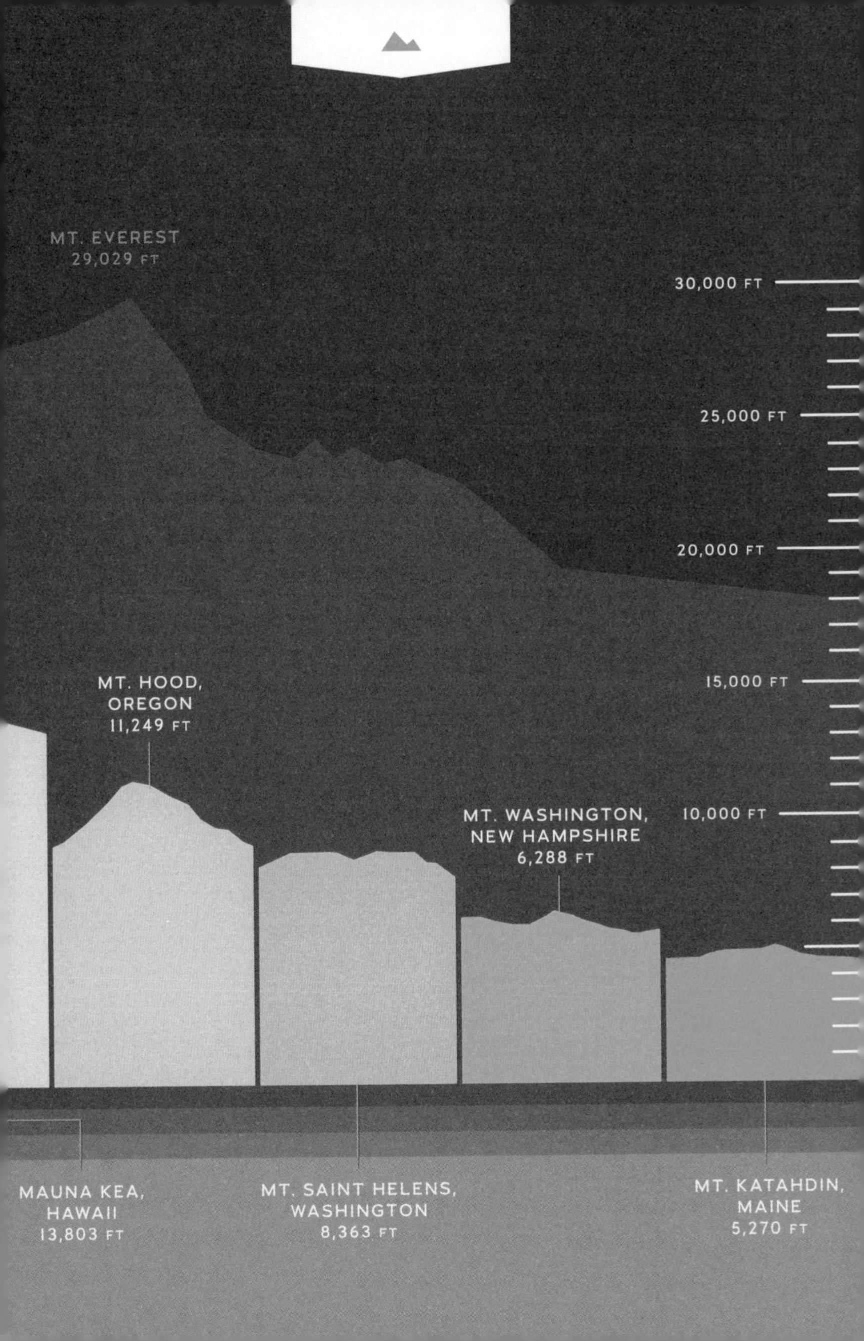

MT. EVEREST
29,029 FT
30,000 FT
25,000 FT
20,000 FT
15,000 FT
MT. HOOD,
OREGON
11,249 FT
10,000 FT
MT. WASHINGTON,
NEW HAMPSHIRE
6,288 FT
MAUNA KEA,
HAWAII
13,803 FT
MT. SAINT HELENS,
WASHINGTON
8,363 FT
MT. KATAHDIN,
MAINE
5,270 FT

HOW TO TAKE GREAT
OUTDOOR PHOTOS

Thanks to modern technology, capturing professional-grade photographs is a skill practically everyone can aspire to. With dozens of ways to share or display your prime pieces of digital artwork, the mission of finding that perfect shot is more important than ever before. Of course, editing and adding filters can lend some magic to a photo, but before you jump to those options, try out some of the photography tips below on your next nature shoot.

WHEN TO USE THE FLASH

In most cases, you should avoid using the flash, *especially* when taking pictures outside. Otherwise, you'll end up with a mostly black image because the camera flash doesn't add sufficient light. Exceptions can be made when you're photographing people, animals, or objects in low light.

HOW TO UTILIZE THE RULE OF THIRDS

When lining up your photo, remember the "rule of thirds." In other words, avoid centering your subject. The same can be said for the horizon or other solid lines like trees and buildings.

Instead, imagine breaking your picture into thirds (both horizontally and vertically) and placing the subject along one of the gridlines. (Most digital cameras even offer a grid overlay as a viewing option.) When your subject is off to the side instead of dead center, the result is more appealing and allows the eye to travel across the frame.

Sometimes, for effect, this rule can be ignored—as in the case of a road or a bridge that leads the eye straight through the image—but it is important to know the rule before you break it.

HOW TO FRAME YOUR SHOT

Try to frame your photo naturally, perhaps by using leaves, a tunnel, or a doorway to emphasize the subject. Don't let the frame steal the attention from the subject. Remember that a subtle approach can lead to the most beautiful results.

WHEN TO CAPTURE THE BEST LIGHTING

The best outdoor photographs are often taken during the Golden Hour, shortly after sunrise and shortly before sunset. The lighting during this time is softer and redder than it is when the sun is high overhead. You will also avoid harsh glares and stark shadows when the light is lower and more diffused.

HOW TO MAKE THE MOST OF THE MOMENT

Even though great photos are easier to take than ever, don't make the mistake of walking around with a lens plastered to your eye. Too many people choose to see nature only through a screen—even when they're in nature! To avoid that, take some time to view and appreciate what you're looking at before you start snapping photos. *Enjoy the real thing.* Chances are you'll discover a fantastic angle that you wouldn't have noticed otherwise.

HOW TO USE MANUAL SETTINGS SUCCESSFULLY

Although many cameras now default to automatic settings, it can be fun to experiment with manual settings (aperture, shutter speed, and ISO), which allow you to control all aspects of your resulting photo. Each setting affects the other, so be sure to play around with your camera. That's the best way to learn!

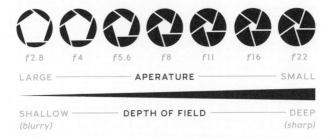

f2.8	f4	f5.6	f8	f11	f16	f22

LARGE ——————— **APERATURE** ——————— SMALL

SHALLOW ——— **DEPTH OF FIELD** ——— DEEP
(blurry)   *(sharp)*

Aperture (or **f-stop setting**) refers to the size of the opening of the lens. F-stops typically range from $f/1.4$ (large amount of light) to $f/22$ (small amount of light). The smaller the number, the greater the amount of light let in (i.e. a wider aperture). One of the most notable effects of experimenting with aperture is with depth of field. The more light let in, the shallower the depth of field, and the more the background appears blurred.

Shutter speed, or exposure time, refers to how quickly
the shutter of the camera opens and closes again when
snapping a picture. This is especially important when
trying to photograph moving objects, which are more apt
to blur at slow settings. So, for capturing wildlife during
daylight, you might want to be ready with a fast shutter
speed. But when photographing still objects, you can
select a slow shutter speed. You can also be creative when
photographing the same object at different shutter speeds.
For example, shooting a waterfall at fast shutter speed will
"freeze" the water in place; shooting the same waterfall at a
slow speed can produce an artistic blurred water.

While **ISO** traditionally refers to film speed, digital cameras still employ ISO settings as a measure of the sensitivity of the image sensor. The higher the ISO, the more you'll be able to capture images in darker settings. So in bright sunshine, you'll want a low ISO (100 or 400), but on cloudy days or other low-light situations, you'll want a higher ISO. However, it's important to know that higher ISO photos can come out grainy.

WHAT ARE CAMERA MODES?

Most digital cameras are equipped with at least these four modes: Program (P), Shutter Priority (Tv) or (S), Aperture Priority (Av) or (A), and Manual (M). Many have additional modes, such as Automatic, Portrait Mode, Macro Mode, Sports Mode, and Bulb Mode. To learn more about shooting modes, use each different auto mode on the camera. Take notice of the settings in the viewfinder as you take an image as this will help you understand how shutter speed, ISO, and aperture affects every photo!

If you'd like to dive a little deeper, here are a couple of books you might find helpful:

* *Digital Photography: An Introduction* by Tom Ang

* *National Geographic: The Ultimate Field Guide to Landscape Photography* by Robert Caputo

CAPTURING MY ADVENTURES

Use the following pages either to sketch or
to mount photos of your experiences.

GET OUTSIDE

Unless otherwise indicated, all Scripture quotations are taken from
the Holy Bible, New Living Translation, copyright © 1996, 2004, 2007.
Used by permission of Tyndale House Publishers Inc., Carol Stream,
Illinois 60188. All rights reserved. Scriptures quotations marked (NIV)
are taken from the Holy Bible, New International Version®, NIV®.
Copyright © 1973, 1978, 1984, 2011, by Biblica Inc.™ Used by permission
of Zondervan. All rights reserved worldwide. www.zondervan.com.

ISBN 978-0-525-65407-0

Published in the United States by WaterBrook, an imprint of
Random House, a division of Penguin Random House LLC, New York.

INK & WILLOW® and its colophon are registered trademarks
of Penguin Random House LLC.

Printed in China
2021—First Edition

10 9 8 7 6 5

SPECIAL SALES

Most Ink & Willow books are available at special quantity discounts
when purchased in bulk by corporations, organizations, and
special-interest groups. Custom imprinting or excerpting can
also be done to fit special needs. For information, please e-mail
specialmarketscms@penguinrandomhouse.com or call 1-800-603-7051.